Leadership:
It's Not That Hard!

Lucas Chang

iUniverse, Inc.
Bloomington

Leadership: It's Not That Hard!

iUniverse books may be ordered through booksellers or by contacting:

iUniverse
1663 Liberty Drive
Bloomington, IN 47403
www.iuniverse.com
1-800-Authors (1-800-288-4677)

ISBN: 978-1-4502-6764-9 (pbk)
ISBN: 978-1-4502-6765-6 (ebk)

Printed in the United States of America

iUniverse rev. date: 12/23/10

For Judy, Keira and Leah. You make me proud every day
– I hope I have done the same today.

Table of Contents

Preface

I have been fortunate to have spent time working with people in leadership capacities across many industries and levels. Going back to my days spent organizing youth leadership camps, to more recent career experiences in banking, transportation, government (Canadian federal, provincial and municipal), and telecommunications, I have seen leaders of all shapes, sizes and styles in action.

One realization that struck me was that very few companies train their people how to be an effective leader. Companies will take their best and brightest "doers" and promote them into roles to lead people, but don't do anything to help the recently-promoted to shift their mindset from "I do the work" to "I inspire others to do the work." Compounded over time and promotions, many companies are led by teams of people who are managers (administrators) but not leaders (inspire others).

Judging from the popularity of "how to be an effective leader" literature, speakers and courses, I'm not the first person to arrive at the "we manage but don't lead" conclusion.

I suspect that this plethora of material only adds to the problem. For the person starting in their first team leader role (for example, my first leadership role involved leading a team of one), even knowing where to begin to sift through the volume of material and gather a few tricks and tips would itself be a lengthy research project.

So, in most cases when it comes to leadership, we either say too little or we say too much. Either way, the result is that many people in leadership roles learn on the job. Some people figure it out, but many do not.

Hopefully this book will help those who struggle with where to begin, by demystifying the basics of leadership. My perspective is that good leadership is rooted in common sense and a respect for people. I've highlighted the elements of common sense and respect that have worked well for me, or that I've seen work well for others. The examples from popular culture are deliberate, intended to illustrate both the relevant leadership observation as well as the "it's not that hard" spirit.

Inevitably, you will disagree with some of my ideas, which is wonderful as challenging my opinions will only help you refine your own leadership philosophy and style, in turn helping you become a stronger leader.

Whether you agree with some or most of my opinions, I hope you enjoy this book and find it helpful in your own leadership journey.

Lucas

Recommended Pre-Reads

After Steve Rogers was assassinated, Bucky Barnes quickly assumed the mantle of Captain America. It made sense – he trained and battled beside Cap during World War II and he knew what Captain America meant to America. He was also scared senseless, as he faced the pressure of being the one man who everyone looked to, to make it all right.

In between moments of self-doubt and panic, Bucky has been figuring it out. He has climbed the Captain America Learning Curve while at the same time figuring out how to be a hero and a leader to those around him. He's not perfect, but he's getting better.

Bucky's experience of having leadership shoved at him, followed by moments of intense panic and "figure it out as you go along", is a parallel for many people growing into larger leadership responsibilities….

To ensure maximum benefit from reading this book, we[1] would strongly recommend you take the time to complete some pre-reads to familiarize yourself with the examples that will be cited in the book. This might take some time, but this will be one of the more interesting research projects you will do in your lifetime.

TV / Movies:

- The Best of Mr. Bean
- Cars
- Forrest Gump
- GI Joe: The Rise of Cobra
- Minority Report
- Monsters Inc
- Peter Pan
- Star Wars: A New Hope
- Star Wars: Return of the Jedi
- Star Wars: The Empire Strikes Back

---

1   The use of the plural first person is indicative that, while this book was written by one person, the deep insights contained therein are worthy of two people.

- Toy Story
- Transformers More Than Meets the Eye
- Transformers the Movie
- WWE shows (particularly from the late 1980s and late 1990s)

Books and other fine literature:

- Calvin and Hobbes
- Dark Avengers
- Dark X-Men
- Secret Invasion
- X-Force
- X-Men, particularly issues in 2009

Also, give P90X a try – the results are quite amazing.

If you're not able to do the background preparation, you will still enjoy and gain from reading this book. Best of all, you will have a pre-set reading list for your next vacation.

Thanks...

To Blake Hanna and Steve Lew for showing me how to inspire while being genuine to yourself.

To the Project Planning and Delivery teams I have supported, for allowing me to learn and refine my own style.

To Blaine Kideckel, David Martin, Glenn Lau, Ian Cruickshank, Jamie Clerf, Jeff Warkentin, Jenn Refvik Bramley, Kristin Bolstad, Mike Giorgio, Nadine Bouchard, Norm Li and Robin Irwin for being wonderful sounding boards for my rants.

To Pat Flewwelling, for opening a door – and showing me how to walk through it - that I didn't know existed.

To Pang Chang for allowing me to grow up watching a true leader in action every day, and to Sumi Chang for showing me how a good leader needs strong behind-the-scenes support.

And most of all, to Judy Chang for putting up with my inane ideas.

Congratulations!

So, you've decided to become a leader! Maybe you've been ordered to be a leader. Maybe you were made leader because no one else was left. In any case, congratulations and well done. Being a leader can be a complicated undertaking, taking some people years of training, reading and experience to build and hone the skills required to inspire people.

But *you* can bypass all of those years of honing and book buying by continuing to read this book, which has collected a whole slew of pearls in a conveniently-sized repository that you (or a close and caring friend who happens to possess impeccable taste in leadership books) were wise enough to purchase.

Now, before we continue, let's step back and clarify what we mean by "leader". This is important, since you have already decided to be one, and it often helps to understand what you are trying to be. "Hockey player", "bartender" and "fireman" are all roles that come with pretty clear indications of what is entailed. Unfortunately, "leader" does not. An important requirement to be a good leader is to know what a leader is.

Ever the overachiever, the Merriam-Webster Dictionary defines "leader" as:

> *a person who leads: as*
>
> - a) *guide, conductor*
> - b) *(1) : a person who directs a military force or unit (2) : a person who has commanding authority or influence*
> - c) *(1) : the principal officer of a British political party (2) : a party member chosen to manage party activities in a legislative body (3) : such a party member presiding over the whole legislative body when the party constitutes a majority*
> - d) *(1) : conductor c (2) : a first or principal performer of a group*

Maybe starting from the beginning will be a better approach.

The Beginning: What is a Leader?

Simply put, a leader is someone who inspires others to follow. This could be in any context, whether in the office, on the ice, in the field, in a classroom or right at home. A leader can be at any level, at any age and have any title. You don't need to be a Vice-President, or Team Captain, or First Cello, or anything else with a Leader Title to be a leader. Someone on a fundraising committee can inspire others to action without being the chair. Simply put, a leader is someone whom others choose to follow.

It's worth noting the difference between "leader" and "manager". A manager is someone who coordinates the logistics of activities; a leader is someone who inspires activities. Someone can be a manager and a leader (and, while we're at it, any title carrying authority) at the same time, but often the two are confused, especially by the managers who aren't good leaders.

Regardless of context, good leaders share traits that inspire others to follow them. If you think about the people who have inspired you, you'll probably see common traits. Most likely, the inspirational people:

- Knew what was going on
- Were confident in their own abilities
- Knew who to go to for help
- Said stuff that made sense
- Had a knack for thinking ahead
- Wanted each person on the team to succeed
- Had a plan

Sound familiar? Strong leadership, oddly enough, is all about common sense. Look at esteemed leaders like Optimus Prime, James P. "Sulley" Sullivan, and Tony Horton. None of them approached leadership with complicated theorems. Instead, they led using common sense. They each treated people like adults, respected the abilities of those around them and were genuine and consistent.

Leaders need to know themselves well: their strengths, their weaknesses and their motivations. At the same time, they need to know the context in which they are leading, whether it be business, religion, sport, art or Saturday night clubbing. After all, it's pretty tough to chart a visionary direction when you're confused about what is going on. With a strong self-awareness and understanding of context, a leader can go about their business inspiring people to get stuff done and to grow at the same time.

These dimensions can be called Personal Leadership (how well do you know yourself), Business Leadership (how well do you know your context) and People Leadership (inspiring the people). You need to build all three in order to be a strong leader:

Personal Leadership:	Knowing yourself is a key component of strong personal leadership, as it gives you an honest perspective of what you can do well, what you need help doing, and where you are flying blind. As important as knowing yourself is knowing how to apply your strengths and weaknesses to different audiences and situations – in particular, knowing how to adapt your communications style depending on the circumstances and the people around you. Not everyone receives information the same way, so a key skill for a leader is to know how to adapt your style to others.
Business Leadership:	Know what is going on and have a plan. It`s hard to whip up a brilliant, textbook-worthy strategic plan for the ages if you aren't entirely clear what is happening around you. On the other hand, knowing exactly what's happening, but not having a plan, is the stuff of secondary Disney characters and not of a strong leader.

People Leadership:	Leading people usually requires those people to be doing something. If the people are doing nothing, you have to do it all, which is a hallmark of a poor leader. What helps motivate people to do stuff is a vision, a direction, a sense of why the team exists - as the team's leader, you need to define that vision and direction for the team - in a way that makes sense to the team.
	It would also be too easy to force people to do things for you against their better judgment, and then burn them out along the way - so, another key mark of success of a good leader is developing people while they're getting stuff done for you. The goal here is to develop such a strong team that you make yourself irrelevant. Ideally you make yourself irrelevant but your own boss continues to pay you - a win-win situation. You spend your days attending "senior leadership forum offsite meetings", your team is off getting tons of stuff done and maybe even becoming leaders themselves, and your boss is taking all the credit for their work. Everyone wins!

The downsides of missing one or more dimensions are worth noting. Don't know yourself? You could be wandering around generating puzzled looks, endless stories of cluelessness and unwanted comparisons to certain cartoon characters depicting suboptimal bosses with strange hairstyles. Don't know your context? The direction you've charted might not be relevant to the team's situation. Know yourself well and know your context well, but can't find a way to inspire the people? If people aren't following, you're not leading.

Tying It All Together

How does this all tie together? A strong leader has all 3 dimensions, as illustrated below:

People Leadership: Inspire the People

Always develop your team members

Take time to understand what motivates each of your team members

Match assignments to skill sets, desires and developmental needs

Give assignments with meaningfully-large scope

Deliver praise and criticism at the right time and in the right forum

Articulate the team's strategy and objectives

Build your team's trust in you

Create an environment where team members trust each other

Prioritize work for the team, and don't be afraid to say no to low-priority work

Change structure and processes to knock down roadblocks

Personal Leadership: Know Thyself

Know and build around your strengths and weaknesses

Play off of your strengths and push yourself outside of your comfort zone

Be genuine as a leader

Adapt your communication style to your audience and circumstances

Business Leadership: Know Thy Context

Synthesize your knowledge to communicate an inspiring direction

Take informed and calculated risks

Not only does this picture tie the concepts together, but it also should make you feel happy that some thought went into this book, now having seen a chart with a clever application of a basic shape. The rest of this book will explain each element of leadership, complete with examples taken from unusual places.

Know and build around your strengths and weaknesses

This sounds pretty obvious, right? You can't lead others until you know yourself first. To know yourself – your strengths, weaknesses, motivations, likes, dislikes and values - is to know what you bring to the table as a leader. It's easiest to lead when your personal desires and values naturally align with the direction the team needs to take - there is no need for uncomfortable and time-consuming soul-searching as you reconcile different value sets. Similarly, knowing yourself allows you to establish a team which compliments your strengths and weaknesses. Most importantly, knowing yourself gives you self-confidence and it prevents you from taking yourself too seriously. If you know you can recover from a mistake, or if you have addressed a vulnerability, or if you have the next move in mind already, you won't panic when running into a problem.

One approach to understanding yourself is to step back and look at what has gone well and what has gone poorly, particularly over the past year or so, and honestly assess what you did well and did poorly to contribute to the outcome. If you did this or that differently, would the outcome have changed? And, why did you do what you did? Understanding motivations for your behaviors will also be insightful. If you start seeing patterns, you will have a starting point. For example, you may notice that in many situations where something failed, you saw ahead of time what caused the failure, but your emotional appeals couldn't convince the rest of the team to change direction. In this case, you might need to conclude that you have to learn how to share your concerns in a fact-based way. Perhaps you notice that when financial information such as business cases show up, you turn away – but then ideas don't achieve the anticipated benefits. In this case, you might need to accept and subsequently address your discomfort with numbers.

From there, seek out external validation of your starting point. Ask people who work with you, ask your closer friends – if you have access to 360 degree surveys[2], take advantage of those tools. Even better, if you have access to formal diagnostic tools such as Insights, Korn-Ferry or Myers-Briggs, use those as additional data points. The more inputs the better, as the larger data set will improve the quality of your self-assessment. The important step here is validation – don't take one person's view or one diagnostic test as the final word, as you will inevitably miss something or over-emphasize something else.

Once you familiarize yourself with your strengths, weaknesses and all of that good stuff, it's time to do something with that knowledge. Leverage your strengths and shore up your weaknesses!. If numbers scare you, you might take a financial analysis class; if public speaking is not your strength, you could join Toastmasters. The next chapter has some more about getting outside of your comfort zone.

That said, you will likely find it difficult to put off being a leader entirely while you're off doing all of that improving and shoring. It will be helpful to build a team around who compliments your own strengths and weaknesses, so that team objectives can be met. If you have inherited a team and don't feel like setting up a garage sale or otherwise starting from scratch, you will find it helpful to understand your team members' individual skill sets and motivations – more on that later.

Surround yourself with people who possess strengths that happen to be your weakness. Poor math skills? Bring on someone with an accounting or finance background. Strong functional skills but lack industry depth? Bring on someone with years of experience in your industry. An ideas man, but a poor planner? Look for someone who has project management experience. Don't stack

---

2   A 360 degree survey is not as much a survey that resembles the girl from *The Exorcist* as much as a survey that allows people with any organizational relationship to you (senior, peer, junior) to provide constructive development feedback. The benefit of this approach is to expand the sample size, so that you are getting feedback from many people instead of just a few; in turn you will receive more different perspectives. Larger companies usually provide these tools, and they are readily available on the Internet.

the team with clones of yourself – not only will that confuse your family as 4 of you climb out of the car at the end of the day, but your team will not be stronger for it.

Look at Tony Horton - when he set about creating the revolutionary, never-been-done home fitness boot camp program now affectionately known as P90X, he realized that while he was very fluent in overall fitness and conditioning, he didn't possess all the knowledge required to make P90X the product that it needed to be. He played to his strengths (structuring the program, developing the resistance and weight training routines) but consulted with others for routines where he was less familiar (karate, gymnastics, core, yoga and Pilates).[3]

Optimus Prime[4] did the same thing. He surrounded himself with Autobots who had skills complimentary to his own. Optimus was the visionary, the guy with the higher-order objectives in mind, but he left administration to Jazz, security detail to Prowl and medical affairs to Ratchet. As leaders in their own right, Jazz, Prowl and Ratchet knew their own teams well enough to know the details required to support Prime – for example, Jazz knew all of the other Autobots' battle skills and would assemble the right team for the mission. On the other side of the battlefield, Soundwave did the same thing – he knew exactly which cassette was needed to shore up his own shortcomings, whether it was Ravage (ground reconnaissance), Rumble (demolitions) or Laserbeak (air reconnaissance).

As a leader, make sure that your team is stronger than the sum of the parts – ensure everyone brings complimentary skill sets to the table. Start by looking at yourself, and bring on others whose skills are complimentary to yours. If you already have a team in place, you probably should start by working with those individuals

---

3 Tony Horton asked Wesley Idol to help develop the Kenpo Karate routine, Dreya Weber for gymnastics / core, Ish Moran for yoga and Leanne Wagner for pilates.
4 The original Optimus Prime from the so-called "Generation 1" cartoon series. Not the Optimus Prime in the subsequent cartoons, and not the live-action Optimus Prime - Optimus Prime does not have a mouth.

before replacing them – otherwise, they probably will get upset, and you might not have any space for the new people.

Play off of your strengths and push yourself outside of your comfort zone

Now, while you and your complimentary inner circle are working on leading the team to greatness, make sure you take steps to play off your strengths and improve upon your weaknesses. There are a couple of different approaches to this:

- Change yourself
- Change your environment

Experts will typically tell us to focus on changing ourselves, in turn ensuring that Self-Help sections of large bookstores are well stocked. While this inward focus may be admirable, the clever and playful leader knows to pursue self-improvement while concurrently adapting the environment to be favorable to their own realities. In other words, change the world to suit yourself.

This all-out tactic is not unlike Calvinball. For those who focused on their university studies instead of reading *Calvin and Hobbes* books, Calvinball is a game that has no rules save for one – the game cannot be played the same way twice. As such, this game plays to Calvin's strengths (his imagination) and stays away from one of his top weaknesses (can't follow rules). As a result, he finds far more success with Calvinball than, say, lunch-hour school baseball.

Sleight-of-hand is another tactic to alter your environment in order to mask your weaknesses and play to your strengths. Remember the 1990s WWE wrestler Gangrel? If you watched WWE back then, you will. He was the vampire-looking wrestler who entered the arena in a ring of fire with a cool-sounding goth-like song. This set-up played to his strength – he had long fangs. Legitimate fangs. He was dressed up in a frilly vampire-like shirt (reference: Tom Cruise's clothing in Interview with a Vampire). WWE occasionally drenched his opponents in fake blood. He used his vampire powers to seduce Edge and Christian into The Brood. All very cool, which served to mask the fact that he sucked on the microphone and, all in all, was very much 1-dimensional. Yet he was cheered due to his cool factor – illustrating that you can change your surroundings to play to your strengths, even if the list of strengths is one line long and revolves around your teeth.

If you're not able to change the environment to adapt to your weaknesses, you may need to consider improving upon your weaknesses, which typically requires you to push yourself out of your comfort zone. Before we continue, let's explore the alternative: namely, staying in your comfort zone. Why would anyone want to leave their Zone of Comfort? It's so comfortable, it's safe, it's familiar, and it probably has a bar fridge, a nice chair and matching ottoman. Presumably this comfort zone is located in your house as opposed to someone else's house, seeing as this would mean you are in someone else's comfort zone and should probably find one of your own – which, ironically, would push you out of your comfort zone if you aren't used to looking for new comfort zones.

In any event, staying in your comfort zone for too long risks intellectual stagnation, boredom and clothes that pick up just a little too much of your scent. In contrast, leaving your comfort zone introduces you to new stimuli which present new challenges, in turn forcing you to stretch and grow and better yourself (after a period of utter confusion and panic).

There are good ways and bad ways to push yourself out of your comfort zone. Good ways tend to follow some introspection and identification of specific challenges you'd like to overcome to strengthen yourself. You might choose to take that financial analysis course after thinking about it for the past chapter. If you don't understand what teams who you work closely with do, you might want to expand your business knowledge and spend a day with someone from that team. You might start a workout program, if you feel that your confidence is affected by your physical appearance. You might take a power-skating course to improve your performance on the ice. All of these examples are self-initiated and rely on your knowing your weaknesses and desire to push yourself out of your comfort zone.

Bad ways tend to be thrust upon you unexpectedly by people who can immediately and without consequence terminate your employment, frequently accompanied by a "this is your number-one job ticket" speech[5] – due to the limited scope of what you can do in these situations, let's focus on the good ways. Bonus, the more often you push yourself, the more prepared you will be, when someone else pushes you. So let this be a motivation to you, to hurry up and find that uncomfort zone.

Consider Monsters Inc's James P. "Sulley" Sullivan, who successfully pushed himself out of his comfort zone. Sulley, the acknowledged leading scarer at Monsters Inc., inadvertently came across Boo when she snuck into the Monsters Inc. production floor. Despite his initial extreme fear of human children, Sulley grew to appreciate Boo and accepted responsibility for returning her safely to her bedroom. He remained outside of his comfort zone as he overcame challenges from Randall and Henry J. Waternoose to not only successfully return Boo to her home, but also to uncover a conspiracy by Waternoose and take over as CEO of Monsters Inc (and subsequently drive power generation through the roof, via the new source of laughter).

There is such a thing as going too far out of your comfort zone. Take Captain Hook, for example. He's fighting Peter Pan on the ship, then for some reason, he decides to climb the rigging to get the advantage - what was he going to do? Peter Pan CAN FLY. Getting some height is not going to gain Captain Hook the advantage against Peter Pan. Setting a trap in the hold, or using a Lost Boy as bait, or pulling out a cannon – these might have stretched Captain Hook. Instead, climbing the rigging is just is an excellent example of poor planning.

Knowing your strengths and weaknesses will help you understand your limitations and develop an intelligent plan to develop on your weaknesses outside your comfort zone. In the experience of doing new things, you will have opportunities to work on those areas where you are less comfortable. Even better, you might find new skills that you didn't know you had, or notice a pattern of behaviour that you hadn't seen before, or find new opportunities

5   Examples of bad ways could include a budget analysis assignment if you fear numbers, delivering an executive presentation if you don't know the material, or accepting a bull-fighting challenge if you are drunk.

for growth. All of these examples reinforce the need for a good leader to try new things from new angles – with a plan.

Be genuine as a leader

One of the worst things you can do, from a Sybil "keep your personality together" standpoint, is to try and create a leadership persona that is different from your true self. Now, you might ask what a leadership style is, or why you need a leadership persona. You might also ask what is Sybil.[6]

Most successful leaders find and develop a leadership style that is consistent with their own – usually their "in front of the team" persona is a logical extension of their true persona. If they are straight-shooters with their friends, they will be straight-shooters with their team. If they are quiet thinkers in private, they are quiet leaders. Very rarely will you see a successful leader adopt a style that is completely contrary to their true self, which is likely because people will detect the non-genuine style, and no one likes a liar.

No one likes a puppet, either, which is what some leaders sound like when they start shilling the corporate line. Even a corporate toe-the-line type can toe the line without sounding obvious, if they couch the line in a way that is consistent with their own personality. Consider the differences between these approaches:

- "The cadence and momentum we are building right now is palpable and evident across all of our businesses. Indeed, we are witnessing the development of an exciting growth trajectory, which will be augmented by how we leverage the integration of these capabilities to benefit our clients in all of our markets."[7] – OR,
- "We are going to make a lot of people happy by going for it now."

The message is the same in both cases, but the first example builds up mistrust in those hearing the message – mistrust coming

---

6   Starring Sally Field, Sybil is the true story of a young woman who developed at least 13 different personalities. At one point, this was required viewing for anyone considering a future in psychology. For those not pursuing such studies, or simply seeking lighter movie fare that involved Sally Field, might we suggest *Mrs. Doubtfire*.

7   We wish we made this one up.

from a suspicion that you are hiding something or don't have a plan and are incompetent. The latter honestly summarizes the situation without overcomplicating things. People who hear the second message will know what is coming next, and why. Using excessive jargon detracts from your credibility, as you come across as someone showing off your new Buzzword Bingo skills instead of wanting to get things done.

Professional wrestling has many examples of people who successfully built public personas that were extensions of their personalities. As the "Shaman of Sexy" John Morrison says, "It's cool where you can be a character and also be yourself. John Morrison is more like me.... Everyone has a flamboyant part in real life. They have a wild side. In my job, I get to show that wild side. John Morrison is me with the volume turned up."[8] Morrison isn't the only one who says that – Christian, The Rock and Stone-Cold Steve Austin have all made similar comments that they built on their true personalities to create an on-screen wrestling character who was genuine and multi-dimensional.

Going the other way and creating a leadership persona with no basis in your true self carries some risks. As you switch between personalities (think Bruce Banner and the Incredible Hulk), there are likely going to be some inconsistent behaviors. You will probably be uncomfortable trying to be someone else, which will manifest itself in the form of muted passion and enthusiasm. You might use big words to mask your discomfort. The end result will be that people will pick up on the inconsistencies and not trust you as a leader.

The bottom line is that people will pick up on fake and insincerity. Build your leadership style around who you truly are. If you're quiet, don't try to be loud. If you're loud, don't try to be quiet. If you're too loud, you might want to take a few steps back – we can't hear ourselves think.

---

8   Tim   Baines   (Ottawa   Sun,   http://slam.canoe.ca/Slam/ Wrestling/2010/02/19/12955771.html)   interview   with   John Hennigan, "John Morrison is me with the volume turned up".

Adapt your communication style to your audience and circumstances

Different people appreciate different communications styles. Different situations demand different communications styles. Good leaders are able to adjust their communications style to adapt to their audiences and situations. If this obvious series of statements were truly obvious, we wouldn't need this chapter. The unfortunate fact remains that this isn't obvious, and there are many leaders who put their head down and just shove out those communications to whoever and whatever is nearby, just sweating out those messages and hoping against hope that someone will interpret the pontifications as they were intended. The results have been less than stellar. The entire game of "Telephone Tag" was developed to show children the shortcomings of the "Sweatin' Out the Oldies" style of communications.

Instead of being seen as a pool of sweat to be sprayed at all, communications style is more like a toolkit, where you pick and choose what you need based on the situation and the audience. You might find that you need to take a different approach to get people to understand and agree to your point. Audience not taking to an Imperial Edict? Try softening your approach. Ask leading questions, make a few jokes, smile a bit more. Maybe the reverse is true and Mr. Nice Guy isn't getting the point across. Time to lay the verbal smack down and be crisper in your points. Large meeting rooms aren't the best places to introduce a new idea, so maybe a pre-meeting meeting to build some key alliances is in order. If anything, flexing your communications style should be fun! Change up your delivery style, the forum, the vehicle, the size of audience. It will be like Communications Roulette, and who doesn't like games? Be plyometric in your thinking!

Examples abound of how style flexing has helped leaders. Woody spent one-third of *Toy Story* trying to make Buzz understand by yelling at him, to no avail. Then he changed it up and started to use spaceman references when they entered Pizza Planet and Bingo! Buzz immediately understood Woody's point and they were off to the races. In fact, Buzz understood so well that he overachieved and raced off into the claw machine with the little 3-eyed alien toys.

Pro wrestling is another good example. For the longest time (and sometimes, one promo interview felt like the longest time back then), wrestler interviews and promos entailed the same formula of:

- Announcer stands on stage with microphone, and introduces the wrestler.
- Wrestler steps up to microphone and launches into a 5-minute tirade about what he was going to do to the other wrestler. Lots of finger pointing ensues. The announcer stands beside the wrestler, looking very much like a piece of household furniture.
- Audience cheers because someone discovers that popcorn just went on sale at the concession stand.
- Wrestler leaves.
- Rinse and repeat.

After a few of these back to back, which was a typical NWA Saturday night, everyone is eating cheap popcorn and thinking about what they want to watch next.

Fast forward to the 1990s, where the Rock and Stone-Cold Steve Austin built audience interaction into their promos – and, in the process, enhanced their appeal to their fans. Neither spent their time yelling into the TV camera. They sang songs ("Smackdown Hotel" and "Margaritaville" haven't been heard on WWE TV since, unfortunately), imitated other wrestlers (Rock's interview where he makes fun of the Undertaker, Rikishi and Billy Gunn still cracks us up), encouraged the fans to chant ("What?") and finish their catchphrases, and even delivered interactive promos from dressing rooms.

Fans loved it – the creativity and the unpredictability got and kept the audience's attention. Both wrestlers still got across their points about being ready to beat up their opponents, but did so in a way that was entertaining and far more appealing to fans than the "yell at me" technique.

So think about that – the next time your message isn't being heard, launch into a catchphrase, sing a little "Margaritaville" and stop pointing at the camera.

Synthesize your knowledge to communicate an inspiring direction

One of your jobs as a good leader is to connect the dots between what is happening, articulate what good looks like, and what needs to happen to get from now to good. Along the way, connect people, so that you unite parallel efforts and resolve conflicts.

To be able to do all of this, you need to know the context in which you are leading. And by context, we are referring to the industry or sport, trends, key players, relevant lessons learned and that sort of thing. Proactive tactics to stay on top of context and best practices (across industries) would include talking to others in the industry, reading trade magazines, joining industry organizations and so on.

One of the key benefits of understanding what is going on to give you a starting point for what you want to do next. And not just a "I want steak sandwiches for lunch" next step, but something big, something visionary, something that excites people. Use your knowledge to identify opportunities to radically improve results, and link all team tasks to broader objectives and direction! For something that ambitious, you really need to know the ins and outs of what is surrounding you, which in turn allows you to intelligently challenge the status quo and drive improvement, whether it be new approaches to old problems, rethinking what is and isn't a priority, or reassessing how you go about getting things done.

Developing a new approach to old problems can be the easiest win – first of all, it cuts in half the amount of work you need. Instead of having to do a bunch of work to find a new problem, then having to do more work to develop a new approach to solve it, you only need to come up with a new approach. If you're in a rush, or if you're not yet sure about this leadership thing and want to try it out before committing, we recommend this option. You might find success with this, build some confidence and then try looking for new problems.

And there are many examples of where people were successful in coming up with new approaches to old problems. Mr. Bean is a leading thinker in this space. Whether it is bringing a fish to the department store to make sure he's got the right pan or test-brushing a toothbrush before buying it, he innovates the shopping experience. By testing the merchandise before he buys it, he eliminates any need for an inconvenient trip back to the store for an exchange – all the more impressive if you consider the operational expense that he's saved for the store, as the cashier (and the cashier's manager, who would provide their approval) isn't required to spend time to process the exchange. In a world where we seek to eliminate unnecessary cost drivers, Mr. Bean's innovative approach is a model for the rest of us.

This entire context isn't as helpful if you cannot tie it together and make sense of it for your team. With this perspective, you can articulate a vision and direction that inspires your team. You can anticipate ongoing obstacles and challenges, and prepare your team appropriately. You can start to build relevant skills within your team, if those are lacking. You can identify duplicate and contrary efforts, and take action to merge parallel work and re-direct opposite initiatives. All of this comes with being able to apply trends and background to set a common direction that all of your team want to follow.

Think of yourself as Tom Cruise in *Minority Report*[9], where he's in front of the projected computer screen and moving pieces around with the fancy gloves. If you need to go change into darker clothing to feel more in the part, please go ahead. We will wait for you.

In *Minority Report*, Tom is moving various pieces around on the screen – connecting stuff here, separating stuff there. That's what you will be doing, in your head. Know of three projects that are doing the same thing? Well, go ahead and let the people doing

9   *Minority Report* is the story of a man who is accused of committing a murder he hasn't yet committed. The crime will allegedly happen in the future. But it hasn't happened yet. This theme of not being able to place events in a particular time will be discussed in more detail in a later chapter.

the projects know, so that they can stop duplicating work and, instead, rearrange their efforts to drive in the same direction. This exercise is even easier if you have a direction in mind, and have already communicated this to the team – this will save on time needed to introduce the vision.

Look at Cyclops, leader of the X-Men. Knowing where mutants had been (numbering in the millions, but often fighting amongst themselves) and where they currently stand (numbering the low hundreds, with growing resentment among the homo-sapien population), Cyclops was able to articulate a vision for survival en route to creating Utopia, a sanctuary for all mutants. Utopia was quickly inhabited by mutants who previously had been allies with as well as enemies of the X-Men. When the Dark Avengers and Dark X-Men attacked Utopia to once and for all eliminate Cyclops, all resident mutants took action to successfully repel the attack.

Use your knowledge and contacts to connect the various dots, and draw clear links between context, vision, strategy and specific actions. Not only will this give your team more background understanding of what they need to do (and why), but it makes for a really cool speech when you need that material.

Take informed and calculated risks

Leadership is rarely about black and white. The reality is that leadership is most needed when navigating through grey zones that bring difficult tradeoffs and consequences. Fortunately, you have already established a lot of context, which gives you sufficient understanding to know when something is a risk and if so, how big of a risk it represents. It's helpful to frame difficult choices in terms of likelihood and impact, and weigh them against benefit.

Likelihood refers to the chance that something (usually bad[10]) is going to happen as a result of a decision. Impact refers to how much the "something" will affect you. Some occurrences will have a high probability but insignificant impact (e.g., it's guaranteed you will receive a dirty look from someone who doesn't like you). Some things will have a low probability, but would have a high impact (e.g., accidentally posting your phone number and Social Insurance Number in your Facebook status update field for all to see). A helpful tool to consider risk is the 2x2 matrix, with the axes being Likelihood and Impact. High likelihood and high impact typically are less desirable than low likelihood and low impact.

The way to approach the matrix is as follows:

- Identify the options you are considering. Sometimes you will need to identify the options that other, senior people are considering as well.
- Plot each option against the "Likelihood" axis and "Impact" axis. It can be helpful to label each option on your chart, particularly if you have more than one option. You might also consider adding a couple of bullets to remind yourself why you plotted them where you did. Failing to do so risks undermining your careful analysis as you appear startled and confused when people ask you for your rationale.

---

10   If you particularly enjoy unfortunate circumstances, "risk" might mean "risk that something good will happen", but you should get the point.

After doing your Likelihood / Impact analysis, you can take that information and weigh it against the benefit of proceeding. Sometimes, high likelihood and high impact will scare you away. In other situations, where the potential benefit is too large to ignore, you will proceed and take steps to mitigate the likelihood and / or impact of any negative consequences.

Let's apply this model to 2 case studies:

Scenario 1: Luke Skywalker is flying just off the surface of the Death Star, looking for that elusive shaft opening. His tracking computer is counting down the meters to the firing point, when suddenly and inexplicably, Luke hears his mentor Obi-Wan "Ben" Kenobi's voice, encouraging Luke to Use the Force. <u>What is the risk if Luke listens to Ben and shuts off his navi-computer?</u>

Framed in the 2x2 matrix, Luke would need to frame the key risk – we might suppose that the key risk was "missing the shot". Impact would be pretty high – specifically, the Death Star would blow up Yavin's moon, where the entire Rebel Alliance was located, which would end the rebellion and kill all of Luke's friends. This would be a significant impact.

On the other hand, the likelihood of missing is up for debate. To anyone who doesn't believe in The Force, the chances that Luke would miss the shot are pretty high. To a Jedi, it's a no-brainer and likelihood is extremely low. Luke, being Jedi-oriented and a fan of Obi-Wan, was inclined to be Force-friendly; as a result, he might consider the risk of missing the shot to be very low. Therefore, the two perspectives would be plotted as follows:

Scenario 1: Risk that Luke misses his shot by turning off his navi-computer

High
Use the Force (Jedi perspective)
Friends and Rebellion die if he misses, but....
Unlikely to miss
Use the Force (Non-Jedi Perspective)
No chance in @#$@# that he will make the shot
We're all doomed!
Impact
Low
Low
High
Likelihood

As it turns out, he was right about making the shot, and 3 years later we were treated to the best movie of the Star Wars series in *Empire Strikes Back*.[11]

Scenario 2: Mr. Bean walks down to the beach with bathing suit in hand, ready for a nice swim. Upon arriving, he encounters a man lounging in a chair. He needs to change, but there are no change rooms nearby. As such, he needs to change in front of the man but without revealing any personal details. <u>What is the risk that Mr. Bean will inadvertently flash the man if he changes into his bathing suit, while on the beach?</u>

Impact of Mr. Bean's inadvertent reveal would be embarrassment on Mr. Bean's part, and maybe abject laughter on the part of the other man. Maybe he would faint. Who knows exactly how he would react? Mr. Bean might be too hard on himself, and the other man might enjoy himself. In any event, we can say that the

11 In descending order by quality, the Star Wars movies would line up like this: *Empire Strikes Back, A New Hope, Revenge of the Sith, Return of the Jedi, Attack of the Clones* and finally *Phantom Menace*.

impact would be Mr. Bean's embarrassment, and as such, call it "medium".

Likelihood would be mitigated if Mr. Bean could manage to change into his bathing suit in a way that started with his putting his bathing suit over his pants. So, let's say it's a low likelihood. Consider the picture below:

Scenario 2: Risk that Mr. Bean reveals too much

As it turned out, Mr. Bean successfully changed into his bathing suit without revealing anything. As it also turned out, the man on the beach was blind. Had Mr. Bean known this, his matrix might look like this:

Scenario 2a: Risk that Mr. Bean reveals too much

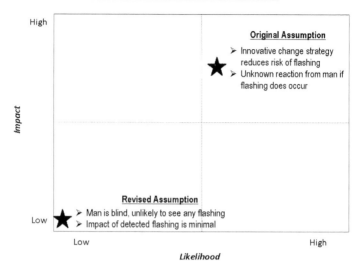

Therefore, the opportunity for Mr. Bean in this situation would have been to gain additional context before acting.

To prepare yourself for your leadership role, you may want to apply this framework to situations facing you today. For your convenience, we have included a blank table below that you can photocopy over and over:

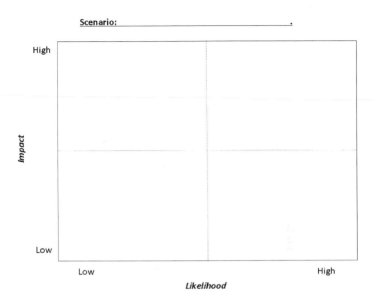

Scenario: _____ .

As a leader, it's critical for you to be comfortable with the idea of taking risks. Don't be afraid to make mistakes, but know how to improve the quality of the risks that you and your team take. To avoid taking blind risks, we would recommend you approaching risks with some framework in mind, like the one we have just introduced. Using an approach like this will give you the added benefit of being able to share your assumptions and thinking with those around you, as opposed to keeping everyone in the dark. And keeping others in the dark is typically not an effective leadership technique.

Always develop your team members

Now that you've ascended to a leadership role, what is your first course of action? Well, you should develop a succession plan. Now, this might strike you as unintuitive, and you might be saying to yourself, "I just got here! Why am I already supposed to think about my successor?"

Naming and developing a successor (and in turn, successors to your successors) isn't a once-a-year and when-you're-ready event. It should be something that you keep top of mind – not just to ensure you are giving people appropriate opportunities to grow and learn, but also to make sure you live the Golden Goal of Leadership (make yourself irrelevant by building a strong team, and without being useless) everyday. If you are focused on making yourself irrelevant, you will properly elevate the team in ability and in profile. If you don't have this focus, you will lapse back into doing things for the team and becoming essential to day-to-day operations, which is exactly the opposite of becoming irrelevant.

As an aside, some of you might worry that this kind of "make yourself irrelevant" verbiage is encouraging leaders to abandon their teams – not true. Instead, we strongly believe that a leader who, by doing the right things to build their team en route to making themselves irrelevant, will not abandon the team simply because people-inspiration is ingrained in their DNA. Someone who gets as far as building a strong team with multiple successors and a career path for each and every team member will not be capable of not caring anymore, no matter how self-sufficient the team becomes. The leader will have invested so much of themselves in the team's success that they will want to see the team succeed, which is difficult if the leader outright abandons the team. They will, at a minimum, check their Blackberry for updates while on at the resort.

The first step to developing a proper succession plan is not, contrary to popular belief, identifying a successor. No, it is more basic than this. You need to accept and believe that building a strong successor – or, if you are lucky and enjoy a little controversy, multiple successors – isn't a threat, but rather, it's good for business, and good for you. To the last point, if you develop strong successors, you will be commended for having an incredibly-strong team from top to bottom, and find yourself on vacations not needing to worry about how things are going, since your incredibly-strong team will be managing in your absence.

An apt metaphor here is how a strong villain makes for a strong hero. Optimus Prime and Megatron. Spider-Man and Norman Osborn. The X-Men and Magneto. The X-Men and the Sentinels. The X-Men and Apocalypse (the X-Men need to lighten up). The Fantastic Four and Doctor Doom. Captain America and the Red Skull. Batman and Joker. Superman and Lex Luthor. Mr. Bean and the Turkey. In all of these examples, the stronger the villain, the stronger the hero when they eventually triumphed. Conversely, a hero doesn't appear stronger when they defeat someone who has trouble rolling out of bed in the morning. From a leadership standpoint, a leader is only as strong as the entire team – a leader of a weak team probably isn't a great leader. So the lesson here is to take all opportunities to build up your team - in turn, you will appear more successful as well.

So go ahead and identify a successor. Usually they are on your team, or near your team, or you know them to possess the right skill sets. Randomly selecting people from a police line-up is not recommended, not even if you lead a criminal organization, as the people in line were not smart enough to evade capture. The skills that this person possesses should largely meet the needs of the role you are in. You might even consider talking to them, to confirm that they would be interested in being considered a successor to you. While this may sound awkward and the stuff of high-school love relationships ("Do you, um, want to be my successor?"), the talk is a good idea in case the person you have in mind aspires to be something other than your successor, which would be an awkward situation if you announced their promotion to your role and they had left already.

Working with the person you have in mind, you probably want to honestly assess strengths and weaknesses, and work out a plan to build on the strengths and improve on the weaknesses. Optimus

Prime built up Ultra Magnus, by putting him in charge of Autobot City, as part of his plan to name Magnus as the next Autobot leader. Ultra Magnus had full reign of the operations, and had help from strong lieutenants (Arcee, Kup, Perceptor, Blaster, Springer) to ensure he had freedom to lead and grow. In fact, Prime's last act was to pass the Matrix of Leadership on to Ultra Magnus.[12]

The added benefit of building up a successor is opening up new opportunities to delegate work under the guise of "development". Some might believe "delegating work" is also known as "shirking responsibility"; but when you give a successor an chance to stretch their wings, it's properly called "developing your people`.

A couple of other factors must be observed, as you build up a successor. First, don't hoard the glory. Stepping back and letting someone else lead is undermined when you swoop in at the end and claim all of the hard work and accomplishment was your own. The first problem with this approach that you miss the opportunity to make your successor (and team) look stronger in others' eyes. The second, and equally-as-problematic issue here is that you then invite requests for status updates by others. A side benefit of giving others their proper glory and due is that they become the first choice for others who seek progress reports and follow-up requests. If you successfully put your successor over (when it is deserved), you can elevate them and free up time for yourself. This is truly a win-win situation.

Consider a lesson from wrestling. Top wrestlers put their opponents over – that is to say, make them look good – even if they themselves are slated to win. Bret Hart was booked to beat Stone Cold Steve Austin at Wrestlemania XIII – at the time, Bret was an established headliner and at the top of the WWE, and Stone Cold was a rising star. Instead of ending the match with Bret cleanly beating Austin and ending their feud, the wrestlers finished the match with Austin passing out in Bret's signature submission move. In the process, this elevated Austin for not giving up and accelerating his journey to becoming the one of the most successful wrestlers in

---

12   He then got attacked and killed by Galvatron, but Galvatron had the advantage of surprise and the Power of Unicron, so it was never a fair fight.

history. In other words, Bret elevating Austin helped create 2 stars out of the match, not just one. Had Bret claimed the glory in the match for himself – by showboating, by demanding an outright win, by doing anything to weaken his opponent – he would have compromised Austin's credibility while at the same time, reducing the value of his own victory.

Actually, before you go to the next page, there's a concept worth dwelling on a bit longer: public endorsement. Whether it was Edge teaming with Hulk Hogan, Triple H taking on Sheamus at Wrestlemania, or any of Hulk Hogan's opponents who were built up for the months leading up to their match, Edge, Sheamus and Bad News Brown / King Kong Bundy / Big Bossman all gained credibility and legitimacy from being treated seriously by established stars. Your own implicit endorsement of your successor - by letting them lead, by publicly accepting their direction, by not putting them down in front of others - will reinforce their legitimacy with others.

So you, as the Bret Hart of Leadership, can approach building up successors in your own world. Work with your successors to build on their strengths and shore up their weaknesses - whether it's by giving focused coaching, tailored assignments to improve the weaker areas or specific training. Know when to step back from the limelight and let others lead - they will build their confidence, others will become more confident in their leadership, and the day that you can slip out the back without anyone knowing is a just little bit closer.

Take time to understand what motivates each of your team members

As a busy leader, it might become tempting for you to make assumptions about what motivates your team. You might assume that everyone wants more money, or promotions, or to work on the sexiest project in the company. You might assume that everyone wants training or to work from home or to be a manager. You might even go the extra step and sponsor your entire team to go through Myers-Briggs, Korn Ferry or other such personality diagnostic assessments. These steps might be very welcome, and compared to other busy leaders who believe that their teams desire to wait on their leaders hand and foot, this represents some advanced thinking for a leader. Bravo!

Sadly, it's not enough to stop there, as generalities and surveys need to be validated with the proper context. Might we suggest investing a bit more time with each of your team members. Spend the time to dig below the surface, and truly understand what makes each team member tick. Tip: this is particularly important if the team member in question tells you point-blank that your surface-level impressions and diagnostic findings are incorrect.

The benefit of this exercise is premised in the reality that not everyone is motivated by the same things. Let's look at three broad categories that motivate people:

- Financial compensation: Along with car, one of two measurements of success for most people. Includes:
    - Salary / wage increases
    - Overtime pay
    - Performance bonus
    - Gift cards and other financial recognition
    - Company vehicle

- Rewards and recognition: Public and private shout-outs for a job well done. Ideally recognizes things that the team member believes warrants recognition. Includes:
    - Promotion / fast track / succession planning

- o Public "thank-you" emails, posts and mentions
- o Opportunities to present to senior leadership or acknowledged and respected experts in the organization
- o Paid vacation and lieu days
- o Being asked to mentor others
- o Inclusion in Management Fast Track program
- o Company vehicle - yes, this appears twice, but company cars can be viewed as both a financial reward as well as recognition

- Self-actualization: Opportunities for someone to remain challenged (in a good way – not in a "I am completely confused" way) in their job by taking on a broader range of activities. Sometimes cynically referred to as "doing more work for no additional pay", and can include:

  - o Specialized training
  - o Job rotations
  - o Job enrichment

Optimus Prime has been successful in understanding the different motivations of his team. He has had to motivate each of Grimlock (likes a fight, wants respect as a leader), Mirage (wants to go home to Cybertron) and Silverbolt (fear of heights) by pushing different buttons. Promoting Hot Rod to Rodimus Prime[13] was a nice touch. And he gave Ultra Magnus (Autobot City), Jazz (Moon Base One) and Grimlock (leader of the Dinobots) each job enrichment opportunities along the way.

Similarly, Lightning McQueen took the time to understand what motivated each of the cars in Radiator Springs in giving back to the community. Whether it be buying new tires (from Luigi), getting a paint job (from Ramone), fueling up (with Fillmore) or resetting the town to look like it did during its glory days (for Sally), every one of his gifts targeted something each car deeply valued.

---

13 Transformers the Movie. Rodimus was far cooler in the movie than he was in the subsequent cartoons – he was kind of useless and whiney in the cartoons. Too bad, he started off well. He might have benefitted from reading this book.

Your performance as a leader is stronger, and more valued by your team, if you understand the true motivations of each team member. With that insight, you can reinforce positive behaviors by addressing the specifics of what motivates an individual.

Match assignments to skill sets, desires and developmental needs

Everyone has the potential to excel at something; it's your job as a leader to find that potential, love it, grow it, nurture it, unlock it and turn it into something relevant that helps your team. This is related to, but not the same as finding what motivates your team – after all, you aren't any further ahead with a highly-motivated but incompetent person on the team.

There are many examples of leaders who understand not just what their team members tick, but also how to make each of them superstars in their own spaces. Optimus Prime deployed Hound for reconnaissance, Mirage for spying, Bumblebee for infiltration and the Dinobots for raw power. If he had tried a different approach, say pitting Bumblebee against Devastator, it's safe to say that the Autobots would have been less successful. Similarly, General Hawk assembled the GI Joe strike team responsible for capturing the Cobra warheads with very specific skill sets in mind: Snake-Eyes and Scarlett led the strike, with Heavy Duty doing clean-up, and Breaker came in only when the situation was won in order to set up the communications between Duke, Rip Cord and Hawk.

So how do you, as a leader, approach personal development planning with someone on your team? The picture below outlines how, ideally, the process should go:

- You and your team member would get together to level set and agree on a common perspective regarding his or her strengths and weaknesses.

   o This common perspective would include arriving at a shared view of what they typically do well - could be any of, or none of, structuring a plan, coming up with new ideas, getting other people to agree, complete the financial analysis, etc.

- At the same time, both of you would agree on what they could and should do better.

- Together and separately, you would validate this common perspective by talking to other people who work closely with your team member, maybe do some skill diagnostics, available resources (tools, experts, materials) and reflect on any new or reinforced insights.

- With this careful introspection and thought, you both can explore future career and development paths, and make sure that you have a common view of the 3-year plan as well as the roadmap to get there. You might even revisit the role they are in today to confirm it is the right developmental step

- Then, at regular intervals - maybe twice a year - you would sit back down and make sure you both felt that the plan still made sense, and that it was on track.

The team member owns their own career progression and skills development, and you commit to setting the right expectations with them and supporting their plan. Ideally this discussion is not a time-vacuum one-time chore; instead, if done regularly and honestly, should be an ongoing discussion.

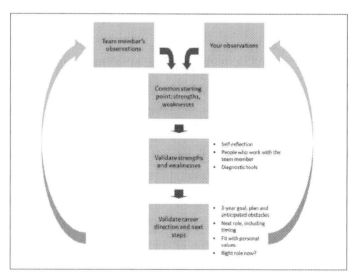

The process is iterative, open and involves both you and your team member. To illustrate, imagine a fictitious discussion between Optimus Prime and Grimlock, the Tyrannosaurus Rex leader of the Dinobots:

> *Optimus Prime:* Well, Grimlock, you've been with the Autobots now for just over 6 months. I think you have a long-term future with the team, and I'd like to make sure we are aligned on what that future looks like. Are you comfortable if we explore that in this one-on-one?

> *Grimlock:* Me, Grimlock, like career planning discussions.

> *Optimus Prime:* Great, Grimlock. So let's look at some of the great things you've done so far. You brought the Dinobots together, after that time you, Slag and Sludge tried to kill us and we had to send Snarl and Swoop to set you straight. That took a lot of leadership on your part.

> *Grimlock:* Me, Grimlock, remember that time. Me munch metal.

> *Optimus Prime:* Yes, Grimlock, that is one of your other strengths - I never have to worry about your ability to bring power to the table. Wheeljack says that you're among the strongest Autobots. On the other hand, are there things you think you're not as comfortable with?

> *Grimlock:* Spreadsheets. Me, Grimlock, hate pivot tables.

> *Optimus Prime:* Grimlock, I have to say, this is one of the most mature career discussions I've ever had. You've been very open about sharing in this discussion - I want you to know how much I appreciate this. Is it safe to say that you agree that your strengths are in leadership and brute power? And, that you don't see yourself as playing a large a role in financial analysis?

> *Grimlock:* Me, Grimlock, say yes.

> *Optimus Prime:* Grimlock, I would like to propose that we keep you as leader of the Dinobots, and keep the team

focused on demolitions going forward. Likely I'd call you and the team in when Devastator showed up, too.

Grimlock: Me, Grimlock, like plan.

Optimus Prime: Also, I would propose that we withdraw your application to the position of Chief Autobot Scientist. I think we can find a couple of alternate candidates - that Perceptor strikes me as quite the clever guy. Is this acceptable?

Grimlock: Me, Grimlock, say yes.

Optimus Prime: Great. Grimlock, again, thank you for such a mature and open outlook. Let's revisit this in 6 months and make sure we both agree things are on track.

Sadly, this process doesn't happen all the time. Some leaders make the mistake of not including their team members in career development discussions, and the actual experience looks like this:

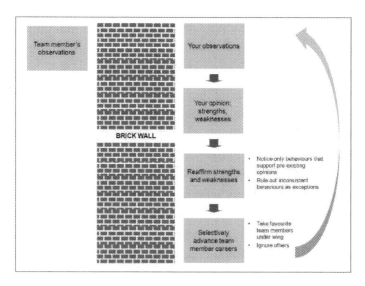

The downside of this approach is that the team member doesn't actually know what you think would be best for them, and in turn, you don't know what they aspire to. Subsequently, the risk is that the team member moves into a role that makes no sense to their strengths, weaknesses or desires. Applying this to the Grimlock example above: Optimus Prime might have moved Grimlock to the Chief Scientist role, which (in hindsight) would not have been a good fit. In short, we recommend including the person in discussions about their career.

Give assignments with meaningfully-large scope

In terms of how leaders hand out assignments, there are two extremes on the style spectrum: outcome-based or process-based. As a leader, you should understand the differences between the two. Outcome-based begins with the premise that an individual possesses the maturity and expertise to figure out a path to success, as long as they are clear about what success looks like as well as any restrictions to how they can achieve success. Little attention, therefore, is given to the specific steps needed to achieve the goal.

Process-based, also known to some as "micro-management", starts with the assumption that the person can't think for themselves and relies on their leader (e.g., you) to figure out all of the basic necessities of life. As a result, they need to have every step laid out for them.

To illustrate the differences between the two extremes, let's take an imaginary but relevant scenario from the fun and invigorating world of budget management – your team's budget, including salary, travel and entertainment budgets, must be cut by 1% by the end of the month. You need to get the wheels in motion with your team immediately. After explaining the situation to your team, which approach are you most likely to take:

- Collaborate with the team to find the most obvious opportunities to meet the budget cutback – eliminate open "to be hired into" headcount, stop unnecessary travel, scale back on team outings. From there, reassess the gap and take more drastic actions if needed, with full disclosure to the team. Share with the team upfront what is in their control and what is outside their control. Make any tough decisions that are needed. Give the team time and space to digest, plan and execute.
- Beef up your Finance and Human Resources team so that they can assign full-time analysts to follow your team's every move in order to scrutinize savings opportunities. Insist on monthly updates for each line item. Complain about low morale.

If you gravitate towards the second approach, you might be suited for senior leadership in a large "legacy" corporation.

Aside from needing fewer HR and Finance people on the team, the added advantage of the first option is that it allows your team to show you their creativity. In turn, they develop their skills and the team grows stronger overall. The key ingredients for this recipe, aside from a competent team, are clear context, known constraints and desired outcomes and timing. With these pieces of information, your team will be set to accomplishing what they need to accomplish – and in doing so, they may not like the situation but will understand the path that they are taking.

Whether you look at Optimus Prime or Woody, there are ample examples of leaders who hand a key outcome to their team and let the team figure out the rest. Optimus Prime assigns his Autobots missions with clear mandates (stop the Decepticons from returning to Cybertron), parameters (don't hurt the humans) and timeframes (they're boarding their shuttle now) – in turn, each Autobot is able to improvise and innovate as needed (Mirage stows away on the shuttle in order to stop it from exiting Earth's atmosphere) to achieve the goal.

Woody sends the army men to scope out Andy's opening of his birthday presents – the team knows where to hide and what to report back to Woody and the rest of the toys, as well as what to do with any unexpected developments (such as the revelation that Andy's mom has a final, secret present for Andy).

The lesson here is that if you let your team think for themselves, they will rise to the occasion and show you that your faith in them was well deserved. Give them assignments that are broad enough and meaningfully-large enough to force them to organize and plan, not just execute and do. Not only will they deliver on the request, but they will likely surprise you with a new approach or fresh ideas that you hadn't dreamed of.

Deliver praise and criticism at the right time and in the right forum

The key to praise and criticism – recognition in general - isn't complicated. At its very basic level, a person has to believe that the praise or criticism is meaningful for it to be effective. This might sound ridiculously obvious, so let's illustrate the point with this example. Someone on your team who we will call Heather has been slaving away at a project for almost a year. Heather has been your prime on this cross-company effort that has required many late nights, countless escalations and building relationships with hostile departments. Her project just launched last week, and it is clear from all around Heather that she carries incredible pride from achieving this milestone. How should you recognize Heather?

- At your team meeting, given that you have a tight agenda, you include Heather in the list of people who are reaching service anniversaries this month. She'll know that you appreciated all of her hard work, implicitly. Besides, doing the project was part of her job anyway, so being mentioned in the team meeting will be recognition enough.
- At your next all-team meeting, which happens to be this week, you take 1 short minute at the top to call Heather out by explaining the project, her role on the project, her importance to the project and to publicly thank her for all of her hard work and congratulate her on this accomplishment. You privately thank her again, and note in that conversation how you have seen her grow and progress over the past year.

Service anniversaries and birthdays are milestones that happen once a year. People typically just need to avoid getting fired or dying to achieve these milestones. As such, people will place less value in recognition of anniversaries than in recognition of things that were under their control – specifically, that they took great efforts to make happen. The lesson here is to recognize what people believe deserves recognition. In turn, when praise and incremental effort (team or individual) are balanced and tie back to what motivates the individual, recognition is valued.

A good leader won't just tie praise to individual motivation, but they will also ensure the recognition is given soon after the good deed is done. When a shout-out is particularly motivating to the person and is delivered in a timely manner, it reinforces the positive behaviour, and the team member will likely strive to repeat or exceed their actions in the future. Waiting too long risks the person forgetting exactly what it was that they had done, and giving recognition that isn't relevant to the individual will fall on deaf ears.

Similarly, criticism needs to be balanced. The team member should believe that their behavior needs to change, they need to agree that the example you are citing is appropriate evidence that the behavior needs to change, and they need to believe that the "what you should have done" feedback is valid and more appropriate than their own actions. If the concern is not limited to a single instance, working a specific plan to address the problem is also an excellent idea. Giving general "you didn't meet expectations" lectures aren't helpful to personal growth, and even worse, tends to leave the person feeling vulnerable and not feeling that they are allowed to make the same mistake (once) in a safe environment. Worse, criticizing in public will put the individual on the spot and leave them defensive, instead of open-minded to listening to the specific feedback. In turn, the person will be less apt to trust you or the team, which will inhibit performance.

Praise or criticism, feedback that you deliver can be more effective if you keep in mind several factors. Keep the message specific and relevant to the individual – they need to know what they did and why the action is worth calling out. The feedback should happen soon after the action has happened, so that the team member remembers what they did, why they did it and the outcomes of their actions. Include a clear call to action – should the person do more or do less of their actions? What is the plan to address a long-standing problem? Finally, praise in public and criticize in private. Public recognition is an ego rush, especially when it happens in front of peers. Criticizing in private will remove the pressure of having to manage others' perceptions, and the individual can focus on the specific point of feedback.

To help you deliver feedback, consider the following table and its examples:

Feedback Component	Do...	Don't...	Examples of Good
Key Point of Feedback	• Person believes what is being called out (praise or criticism) is deserved and appropriate for recognition • Feedback is specific and clear	• Feedback is vague and the person doesn't know what they did wrong • Person thinks what being criticized is trivial	• Optimus Prime names Silverbolt leader of the Aerialbots after he leads the team to victory - which also distracts Silverbolt from his fear of heights
Examples and Call to Action (if any)	• Examples to support content are specific and relevant to the feedback • Actions are specific • If there is a larger plan, it comes with reasonable timelines and clear indicators of success	• No examples are shared • Lecture emphasizes generalities, theories, interesting books or stories about previous jobs • "You should have known better" message lacks specific corrective action to consider next time • Plans and expectations are unclear	• After getting hurt when Autobot Cliffjumper had revealed their presence, Hound asked Cliffjumper not to feel bad about his getting hurt, but for missing Megatron with the shot

Feedback Component	Do...	Don't...	Examples of Good
Timing	• Deliver feedback soon after incident or accomplishment	• Wait until annual review	• Immediately following the destruction of the first Death Star, Luke and Han receive medals in a formal ceremony • Megatron banishes Starscream to an obscure asteroid immediately following a failed coup
Forum	• Public celebration • Private criticism	• No acknowledgement of a job well done • Public criticism	• Tony praises Dominic in Plyometrics right after Dom does intense jump-knee-tucks: "I know how hard that is"

The bottom line is that people will accept criticism and feel good about praise if the message and forum align with their values and perception of effort or severity. General recognition or general criticism will, in contrast, feel less meaningful and be less effective.

Articulate the team's strategy and objectives

Each team should have a purpose and strategy – not simply parroting the broader enterprise (or equivalent, if you're not an enterprise sort of person) goals or citing "the President says" quotations[14], but rather by communicating a strategy and a reason for being specific to the team. Regardless if the broader organizational objective is to sell more stuff, or to help unemployed people in the community by giving them training, or to win the road hockey championship, each team within the organization needs its own strategy and key objectives.

Having this team-specific view helps focus the team on what each member needs to do. The opposite and undesirable effect is to have the team wandering around doing contradictory and unrelated things, which has the negative effect of confusing people, which causes more unproductive meetings, which gets you away from being irrelevant. So, it's important to establish a team strategy and vision to keep the team focused.

For example, the team managing the sales funnel and qualification process might have the objective of ensuring all sales activities are focused on only high-likelihood sales. The supporting strategy would focus on bringing the best qualification practices to drive a 90% close rate.[15] In turn, the team would build processes to ensure that the sales force had insights and data to close large deals. An effective way to frame the team-specific strategy is to ask yourself, "why are we here?" You might consider asking the team this, but we would recommend having some ideas ahead of time; not having any ideas and staring blankly after asking this question might raise strong concerns from your team.

A side benefit of starting from this question is that unnecessary work can be identified and challenged. Should the sales support

---

14   The "My Daddy says" approach stopped working in Grade 3, so it is both fascinating and troubling when senior executives are caught using this to justify their activities.

15   Close rate refers to the number of sales made divided by the number of attempted sales – a measurement of how effective a sales force is performing.

team provide reporting? Sure, if it helps the goal of maintaining 90% close rates; but if the reporting in question is to do with the number of team members trained on the latest ethics course, the team might consider stopping that report. Meeting with sales teams to share information and context is helpful; meeting with finance teams to explain headcount variances is not helpful. Simplifying sales processes is good; overhauling the complaints process is not so good. And so on.

A couple of points of caution, particularly if you are new to the team. Whipping together a team strategy and purpose is an excellent first step, but be careful how you introduce this to the team. You might win a few points for bringing this clarity to the table, but if your strategy implies that the team is made up of a bunch of idiots who have trouble working Velcro, you will lose more points than you've won. Respect that the team existed, and was already doing many things well, prior to your arrival. As a leader, you will need to balance respect for the team's history and past accomplishments with your own vision for the team.

The other consideration is your communications style as you share the team strategy and vision. At this point in the book, we're assuming you've collaborated with your team to arrive at the strategy and purpose; but if you haven't, you may want to do that first. A strategy and purpose are only helpful when people understand and agree with what you are saying. Equally as important as the quality of ideas and insights is the language used in communicating the ideas. Many great ideas have gone nowhere, as the leaders espousing the ideas have relied on jargon and buzzwords to share their "vision". Unfortunately, what the team hears isn't a clear and inspiring vision that compels them to push ahead; instead, they hear that their leader has no clue what is going on, and is hiding behind MBA textbooks and Harvard Business Review articles to justify their position. We would recommend you not become one of those leaders.

A helpful example of a leader who clearly established a team vision and purpose would be Cyclops, who left no doubt why his teams were assembled. Especially as of late, Cyclops has been very aggressive about redefining the role of the X-Men. Under

Professor Xavier, the X-Men were sworn to protect a world that feared and hated them. This entailed reacting to megalomaniacal ambitions of people like Magneto and the Brotherhood of Evil Mutants from time to time, fueled by a team vision and strategy that sought harmony and acceptance by humans. Cyclops' updated take on the team is that the X-Men will protect Utopia, the island home welcome to all mutants – including Magneto and the Brotherhood. Cyclops' X-teams are all focused on protecting mutants from attack, but play different roles to accomplish this goal: the X-Men and New Mutants protect Utopia, Cable trains the mutant messiah and X-Force is the black-ops team to permanently eliminate threats. The respective teams have been successful largely due to their solid understanding of their role in the larger scheme of things. In turn, the individual team members have applied their judgment and context to make the right decisions at every step of their journeys.

So the key lesson here is this: make sure your team knows not only the objectives of the organization at large, but also how their own role and how the team strategy supports that broader objective. As a leader, you have a key opportunity to focus and unite the team by clearly and simply articulating the team's strategy and reason for being. In turn, individuals on the team can use this context to guide their own actions, instead of having to check in at every turn – which, overall, drives growth and satisfaction, as team members know how their day-to-day work is driving towards the overall goals.

Build your team's trust in you

Trust is probably the most important factor that makes someone want to follow another person, yet many people in leadership roles struggle with building and keeping their team's trust. Trust in a leadership setting can be broken out into 2 dimensions – integrity (you do what you say you will do) and experience (you understand the team's work). Both are equally important to keeping your team's trust.

Building trust is a journey where the little things matter as much, if not more than, the big shows of affection. Doing what you say you will do is easy during happy times. If money is falling from the ceiling, it is not difficult to promise that each person on the team will have the opportunity to grab some money. It is more difficult to live up to your promises during challenging times – and it is during these times that your leadership will stand out. The trick during challenging times is to be realistic about your promises and to back up your promises with consistent actions. In turn, it can be helpful to share the broader context with the team, so that they have appreciation for why times are challenging and why you are taking the actions you are taking.

Equally as important is making sure that the team knows you are on their side. Nothing is worse than trying to fight a 2-front battle – getting your job done on the one hand, and doing so in spite of a meddling and two-faced boss[16]. Your team will benefit from the reassurance that, if things go wrong, you will not turn on them and criticize them in public. Private criticisms are both expected and appropriate in light of "you should have known" failure, but doing so in public will only result in feelings of shame and resentment – done repeatedly, this is a virtual guarantee that an expensive team-building event will be needed 6 months down the road.

The perspective here is that failure is step to success. Very few people succeed on the first try, and usually there are growing pains before someone is ready to hit a home run. Before Hulk Hogan was

16 Well, there might be some things worse, like famine, all-day meetings and waiting in the ABM line behind a very confused person, but you get our point.

in movies and on magazine covers, Sterling Golden and The Super Destroyer were wrestling out of small arenas. Before Stone Cold Steve Austin, there was Stunning Steve Austin and the Ringmaster. Before The Rock, there was Flex Kavana and Rocky Maivia. Tony Horton started in the personal training business in 1983, 20 years before P90X was developed. You help your team by allowing them to make mistakes to grow (ideally the same one is made just once, otherwise you need to wonder about learning capacity of the individual in question) and ensuring that they have learned the appropriate lessons from both their failures and successes. Again, make people comfortable enough to fail. If your team doesn't need to worry about your telling everyone else about how useless they are, they can turn their attention to getting the actual work done. Make sure you set the proper expectations with your team, so they know what to anticipate from you, and do what you say.

Highlighting your relevant experience is also key. If you have grown up through the ranks, or bring similar experience to the table, you will be able to speak in your team's language, understand their pains and help them by providing little tips and tricks that you've learned yourself. They will know that your requests and decisions are premised on an understanding of real-world blood, sweat and tears, and not on a book you read last weekend. Equally important, your team will know that, in the event of catastrophic failure, you can step in and, falling back on your previous experience, steer the team back on track. Finally, sharing your experiences with your team will highlight how you learned from your own failures, and what you did to grow from those experiences – valuable perspectives for a team who looks up to you.

Both of these points were very important to Luke Skywalker, when he was struggling to raise his X-Wing out of the Dagobah swamp. Encountering failure a couple of times, he believed that it was impossible to levitate his fighter, and in turn concluded that Yoda was being unreasonable. It was only after Yoda himself raised the fighter that Luke began to believe in The Force, to the point that he took on Darth Vader twice and the Emperor. While there is a lesson here about pacing yourself, the key observation is that being able to do what you ask your team to do can be very powerful as a leader.

If you don't have experience directly related to what your team does, you will need to find a way to make your own experience relevant to them, or make it up. And, unfortunately, faking experience to a team full of experts is walking the fine line between creative leadership and being an idiot, so tread carefully. As much as is reasonable, link your own experience to what your team is doing, but admit when you don't know something and have a plan to learn. Acknowledge when you're wrong, what you will do to correct the situation and stand by your decision. Even Woody admitted his shortcomings to Buzz.

Create an environment where team members trust each other

Trust between team members is equally as important as their trust in you, their leader. Your role here is to build an environment where the team can build trust in each other. The dimensions of trust will be similar, regardless of whether trust is in you or each other: integrity (each team member does what they say they will do), experience (each team member brings the right skill set to the table to contribute) and interests (everyone is driving in the same direction, towards the same objectives). Similar to what will make the team trust you, between one another, they need to set and meet proper expectations.

The art here is balancing how active you are in team building and stepping back from time to time and letting the team figure things out themselves. If they are able to work through problems and challenges without you, they will build trust in each other faster than if you are around as the crutch. On the other hand, if it appears that they are about to engage in fistfights with each other, it might be time to step in, or at least to bring some popcorn.

A popular option of building trust among the team is to bring in outside facilitators to engage in "team building" exercises. Typically these exercises involve being outdoors, playing with out-of-context items such as parachutes and blindfolds, group hugs and personal revelations at the end of the day. The typical result is that you build a team who can recite the Forming / Storming / Norming / Performing cycle and can handle a parachute pretty well, but who works late for the balance of the week to make up for time spent on the team-building exercise.

A less-obvious place for team building is – hold yourself – where the team normally operates. Instead of outsourcing team building, why not step back and ask yourself what you can do with the team to build trust in each other's intent and experience? For example, quite often, decisions and actions without context will appear crazy and mad – but with the proper background, others will quickly realize that it is the environment, and not the person, that is crazy – thus alleviating any concerns about intent. Experience can be shared in a peer-to-peer exchange of ideas – for example, where self-acknowledged experts present key lessons from their experience to others. Credibility is built and ideas are shared. Your role is to build the structures in which the team can strengthen their relationships – and trust – with one another, and to let them know they have the responsibility to do so at all opportunities. Ask the team for their inputs on team direction (which may wind up informing your executive decision). Share with the team the reality of constraints, but give them freedom to try out and test out ideas that stay within those constraints. Allow them to ask questions of you and of each other, so that over time, they feel that their actions were not wasted and helped enhance the team.

The X-Men benefited from living and training together, as they quickly learned about each other's strengths, weaknesses and behavior under stress – which was facilitated by Professor Xavier's visionary Danger Room, which simulated battleground scenarios in a safe setting – before they went into battle. Similarly, in the WWE, wrestlers work with each other in untelevised shows before battling on TV – this approach helps work out the kinks and build trust between the wrestlers, so that by the time they perform on the national and international scenes, they know what to expect from one another and know that they will not injure one another.

All of these cases, the respective leaders found appropriate ways to not just build their team's trust in themselves (as leaders), but also between one another. Pop quiz: would the X-Men have been a stronger team had Professor Xavier hired a parachute-wielding consultant?

Prioritize work for the team, and don't be afraid to say no to low-priority work

It's been said that people who can predict the future see all things happening, but cannot tell relative timelines. Past, present and future all appear to them out of sequence - it might have happened, it might be happening now, or it might be a future thing. There isn't the ability to attach timeframes to events. This goes some way to explaining why fortune tellers will look at you all confused when they tell you what is going to happen.

Sadly, some leaders are similarly lost in space and time. They want everything in place now, despite the fact that some things require time to set up. Nine women can't deliver a baby in one month.

Unlike the leaders mentioned in the previous paragraph, you will benefit from demonstrating to your team that you understand the phrase "these things take time", based on your appreciation of tenses.[17] More than ever, time is at a premium. People don't have enough time. Even when we've found time, we've found a way to lose it. Every Time-Saving Invention has been accompanied by a Time-Saving Neutralizer – consider:

Time-Saving Invention	Time-Saving Neutralizer
PVR	TV snow
Internet	Facebook
Blackberry	Email addiction
Take out	Working out
End-to-End Ownership	Attend 4 meetings a day
Working from Home	Sunny day and backyard patio

Anything you do that helps your team find more time in the day will go a long way to building credibility as a leader. In fact, just demonstrating that you respect your team's time will be a great start. So with this in mind, it is critical for you to be able to prioritize the team's work, accept the good and bad consequences of not doing lower-priority work, and support the team when others

---

17   As in, present and future

complain about the stopped lower-priority and unnecessary work.

Tip: it is a good practice to avoid ignoring your team when they tell you that they are overloaded and that work needs to stop. They might be dogging it, so it's fine to challenge them to rethink their situation and workload – but, it is expected in this case that you give them some new information to help guide their rethinking (e.g., clarify priorities, emerging strategic priority, reduce scope of a project). Simply asking them to "go away and think about it" is not helpful leadership.

So what should one consider in prioritizing work and saying no to work? For starters, it depends what kind of leader you are. If you aspire to be a "my boss said so" type of leader, this book might not be for you – instead, you should call up your boss and ask them for leadership tips. It will be a rewarding discussion.

If, on the other hand, you prefer to think for yourself, you could consider prioritization criteria like timing, benefit, cost, alignment to strategy, available skills on the team and risk mitigation. The relative importance of those factors will differ, but these tend to be the usual considerations. A helpful tool to approach prioritization decisions is a balanced scorecard. A balanced scorecard allows you to identify the key factors that you will use to prioritize one option over another with relative weightings of each option, avoiding the risk that you will inadvertently treat each option as equal.

To use the scorecard prioritization approach, use the following thought process:

- Identify the key criteria that will drive your decision, which may include:
    - Potential benefit: sales, cost savings, employee happiness, client rave reviews…?
    - Timing: when will this thing happen?
    - Cost: what you would need to spend to make it happen?

- o Alignment to strategy: does a particular item make sense in the broader context of what your team is trying to do?
- o Available skills: do you have access to the particular skilled people who will make this happen?
- o Risks and mitigation: what could go wrong, and what do you plan to do, to prevent the bad things from happening? And, what do you plan to do if they do go wrong?

- Weight the criteria so that they total 100%. While relative weightings between the criteria are important (your most-important criteria should be weighted heaviest against the least-important criteria), exact numbers are less important (40%? 41%? 42%?) as the exercise is focused on relative weightings.

- o Using the criteria above, you might be in a situation where benefit is clearly the driver, regardless of timing or cost. Alignment to strategy, availability of skilled people and risk mitigation are definitely considerations, however.
- o As such, you might choose to allocate Benefit at 40%, equally split the remainder between strategy, skills and risks (20% each) and leave timing and cost each at 0%.

- In some cases, a particular criteria will be a "must-have" – e.g., not satisfying that criteria is a showstopper and the option is not worth pursuing.

- o For example, an option that costs more than what you have in the bank is a showstopper.
- o Eliminate from consideration any options that are showstoppers.

- For each option you are considering, score how the option satisfies each criteria.

- o While you can use any scale (1-10, 1-100, 1-1000), we have found a 3-point scale to suffice, since the point of the exercise isn't to pursue science as much as highlight relative priority between options.

   o   If you use the 3-point scale, use 3 if the criteria is satisfied fully (or close) by the option, and 1 if the criteria is not satisfied at all (or close) by the option.

- For each criteria, multiply the score by the weighting to arrive at the Weighted Score.

   o   A criteria weighted 40% and scored 3 (for being a good fit) would have a Weighted Score of 1.2.

- Add up the Weighted Scores for each option.
- The better option will be the one with the highest total Weighted Score. If one option is higher than the others by a significant gap, that will be your best option.

To illustrate, let's apply an example situation to this prioritization framework. The situation is that Luke Skywalker, having just left the Hoth System, is deciding on whether to rejoin the fleet or to heed the word of Obi-Wan and take a detour to the Dagobah system to visit Yoda. R2-D2 is beeping at Luke to head back to the fleet, and Luke needs to prioritize the fleet or Dagobah.

Option			Head to Dagobah			Rejoin fleet		
Criteria	Weight	Score (H=3, M=2, L=1)	Weighted Score	Comment	Score (H=3, M=2, L=1)	Weighted Score	Comment	
Benefit	40%	3 (High)	1.2	Re-establish the Jedi Order by training with Yoda	1 (Low)	0.4	Better seats in the auditorium if he hurries	
Timing	0%	1 (Low)	0	Won't take long to get there	3 (High)	0	Won't take long to get there	
Cost	0%	1 (Low)	0	Not sure what's at Dagobah – unknown	3 (High)	0	Paid for – nothing	
Alignment to Strategy	20%	1 (Low)	0.2	Off strategy. Nothing about being a Jedi in Luke's Rebel Development Plan	3 (High)	0.6	On strategy	
Available Skills	20%	3 (High)	0.6	Flying is the only activity – Luke is a strong pilot	3 (High)	0.6	Flying is the only activity – Luke is a strong pilot	
Risk Mitigation	20%	3 (High)	0.6	Nothing wrong could happen at Dagobah, right?	3 (High)	0.6	Fly faster; those seats are disappearing fast	
TOTALS	100%		2.6			2.2		

Based on this scorecard, and largely due to the importance of Luke's becoming a full-fledged Jedi Knight, going to Dagobah was a higher priority than rejoining the fleet. And that is what Luke did. He visited Dagobah, did a few headstands, had some scary visions and chased after Darth Vader, which led to a 2nd awkward Leia-Luke kiss.

Feel free to practice and use the following blank template:

Option							
Criteria	Weight	Score (H=3, M=2, L=1)	Weighted Score	Comment	Score (H=3, M=2, L=1)	Weighted Score	Comment
Benefit							
Timing							
Cost							
Alignment to Strategy							
Available Skills							
Risk Mitigation							
TOTALS							

As you can see, not only can you clearly articulate your expectations and rationale by outlining the criteria you use to prioritize work; you can create impressive-looking tables that easily transfer to PowerPoint slides. And anything that can be quickly transferred to PowerPoint is a good thing.

Change structure and processes
to knock down roadblocks

You will find times when, despite your best efforts to influence, coach and cajole your team to success, the structure and environment around you is an obstacle to getting things done. This situation might be difficult to identify, as slow progress due to roadblocks closely resembles slow progress due to incompetence. There are several clues that highlight the presence of roadblocks:

- If the team has been trying a variety of different tactics for 6 months with no success, it's a roadblock[18]
- If people from other teams have run into the same obstacle, especially over the same timeframe, it's a roadblock
- If you yourself have run into the same problem with no success, it's a roadblock
- If the people who are the obstacle admit that they are the obstacle, it's a roadblock

As a leader who is likely under pressure to demonstrate creative thinking, it might be tempting to ignore the team's previous efforts and ask them to "go back and assess options" again, or remind them that "we need out-of-the-box thinking here." This is not recommended, as this approach overlooks the fact that the roadblock exists and that help is needed to move ahead.

Instead of trying to change the team, it is appropriate in these times to focus on the environment in which the team operates. Most of the time, the root cause of a problematic environment is not the presence of simple and logical processes and structures; the opposite tends to be true. Pop quiz: does adding more leaders and layers in an organization (a) streamline and accelerate work, or (b) increase the number of status report requests? Changing the environment, whether it be connecting people or streamlining processes, is usually needed because the environment has become too complicated and has lost any ability to be responsive to the organization's needs.

---

18 "Insanity: doing the same thing over and over again and expecting different results." Albert Einstein.

A common-sense approach to knocking down roadblocks would start with tracing what your team does, how they do it, and where they most commonly run into roadblocks. Based on that preliminary view, you can begin to systematically remove those obstacles. Can't get anything done because archrival anti-mutant enemies keep coming back from beatings? Set up a black ops squad to once and for all eliminate these groups, like Cyclops did. Can't get anything done because black ops squads are popping up? Set up your own Dark X-Men force, like Norman Osborn did. Key obstacle is a complex, united front that blocks any attempts to invade Earth? Secretly infiltrate Earth's heroes to sow doubt and mistrust, then launch a massive attack from space and from within to overcome the ranks.

There are a couple of key things to remember here – one, know how to differentiate perceived team incompetence from genuine environment roadblocks. Two, it is important to remember to give your team time to start running again, once you've knocked down the roadblock. Progress will not be immediate, as the team will need time to adjust to the new environment before plodding ahead. Make sure you give them time, or else you yourself will risk being a roadblock.

Bringing It Together

In the end, leadership isn't about magic, secret formulas or titles (especially titles). Good leadership is largely based on common sense. The underlying gist of the points in this book are all common-sense concepts.

Treat people like adults, and they will respond and behave like adults. Whether you are at the top or on your way to the top, show people respect and assume that everyone has the potential to succeed in the right role. On the other hand, micro-manage them and treat your team like children, and they will also respond in kind. If you give them space to exercise their own judgment, to learn from their successes and failures, and celebrate their successes properly, they will respond by taking accountability for their role on the team, their actions and their decisions.

A good leader is multi-dimensional, and brings with him a mix of strengths. He will know enough about his immediate context or business to have an informed opinion. In many cases, he will have risen through the ranks and learned the ins and outs of the business – but being a good "doer" isn't in of itself enough to make a strong leader. A good leader will know themselves well and be comfortable with what they see in the mirror. Their ability to view themselves objectively and humbly sets them up to view their team and circumstances from a realistic perspective. In turn, strong background and balanced perspective aren't enough, if the leader can't find ways to inspire the team that he leads. Leadership is the culmination of all the dimensions of personal knowledge, contextual knowledge and inspiring other people.

The analogy here is of what makes for a successful wrestler. None of Hulk Hogan, Ric Flair, The Rock or Stone Cold Steve Austin would top anyone's list of technical wrestlers. And, while all four are big talkers, there are other wrestlers with equal prowess on the microphone – yet, those other wrestlers have not been as successful as Hogan, Flair, Rock or Austin. Physically, there are many other wrestlers with more chiseled bodies – but those other wrestlers also have not been as popular. What sets those four apart? The combination of wrestling ability, creative innovation and strong personalities helped them build close rapport with their audiences. They found the intangible dimension of inspiring audiences, partially by doing the little things in and out of the ring – facial expressions, body motions, interview styles.[19]

That's another thing to keep in mind: people will notice the little things that you do, so in turn, you should make sure you are paying attention to the little details in your own actions. A couple of things here – first, "good" is defined as "aligned to your individual team members' values and expectations". If you do things that you believe are noble but your team doesn't care for, you will not build credibility in their eyes. Equally important, ongoing and consistent demonstration of good behavior is far more credible than a big one-off show. The more your team sees you behaving all the time in ways that they can understand and, ideally, admire, the more credibility you will build with them as an effective and trustworthy leader. The opposite is true, too. Inconsistent behavior, behavior that isn't aligned to your team's expectations, or behavior that is not genuine – all of these will erode your credibility with your team.

Finally, have fun. People tend to follow other people who are having fun. This is not a surprise. You would expect the same in your personal relationships with friends and family. Someone who consistently does what they say, consistently says things that resonate with you and your values, and is fun to be around, is likely to be someone you choose to associate with for a long time. If you make a mistake or if something doesn't go according to plan, have confidence that you and your team will figure it out, laugh it off and move on. Don't waste your time dwelling on what might have been – have fun focusing on what could be.

As a no-charge bonus, exhibiting the leadership described above will not just improve your standing with your immediate team, but it will also build credibility with those who you depend on and work with to accomplish your objectives. So following common sense that stems from a balanced perspective across yourself, your

---

19 You might bundle all of this under the umbrella "charisma", but that glosses over the individual attributes that make someone charismatic.

context and inspiring others will build and nurture the relationships you have with people in and outside of your team. The litmus test is whether you are recognized as being an important part of others' networks. Do other people want you in their own personal networks? And if you have strong networks, you can get more done, which helps you and your team meet your objectives.

Leadership is a privilege and not a right. Just because you have a title doesn't mean that you have earned credibility with your team over the longer term. In fact, hiding behind your title, and not taking steps to build personal credibility with your team, can hurt your credibility in the long run. You might approach your leadership journey with answers to the following questions in your mind:

- When you eventually move on to another role and leave the team, will your team miss you?
- Do others wish out loud that you were their leader?
- Down the road when they're talking to their friends and colleagues, will your team members cite you as a "I'm so glad I worked for them" leader?

Fortunately, being a leader who deserves "yes" answers to all three questions isn't complicated. It's a lot of work, but it's also pretty straightforward – just use your common sense.

Works Cited

Bendis, Brian Michael., and Mike Deodato. *Dark Avengers*. [New York]: Marvel, 2009. Print.

Bendis, Brian Michael., Leinil Francis. Yu, Mark Morales, Laura DePuy, and Chris Eliopoulos. *Secret Invasion*. New York: Marvel, 2009. Print.

Bloom, George A. "More Than Meets the Eye: Part 1." *The Transformers*. 1984. Television.

Bloom, George A. "More Than Meets the Eye: Part 2." *The Transformers*. 1984. Television.

Bloom, George A. "More Than Meets the Eye: Part 3." *The Transformers*. 1984. Television.

Carey, Mike, John Byrne, Cary Nord, M. A. Supulveda, Dave McCaig, Joe Caramagna, Chris Eliopoulos, John Byrne, Christie Scheele, and Joe Rosen. *X-Men*. New York: Marvel, 2009. Print.

Cars. Dir. John Lasseter and Joe Ranft. By John Lasseter, Joe Ranft, Dan Fogelman, Kiel Murray, Phil Lorin, Jorgen Klubien, Owen Wilson, Paul Newman, and Bonnie Hunt. Prod. Darla K. Anderson. Buena Vista Pictures, 2006. DVD.

Curtis, Richard, Robin Driscoll, and Rowan Atkinson. "The Curse of Mr. Bean." *Mr. Bean*. 30 Dec. 1990. Television.

Curtis, Richard, Rowan Atkinson, and Robin Driscoll. "The Return of Mr. Bean." *Mr. Bean*. 5 Nov. 1990. Television.

Forrest Gump. Dir. Robert Zemeckis. By Eric Roth. Perf. Tom Hanks, Robin Wright, Gary Sinise, Sally Field, and Mykelti Williamson. Paramount Pictures, 1994. Film.

GI Joe: The Rise of Cobra. Dir. Stephen Sommers. By Stuart Beattie, David Elliot, Paul Lovett, Michael Gordon, and Stephen Sommers. Perf. Sienna Miller, Byung-hun Lee, Ray

Park, Marlon Wayans, Dennis Quaid, Channing Tatum. Paramount Pictures, 2009. Film.

"The Key to Vector Sigma, Part 2." *The Transformers.* 1984. Television.

Kyle, Craig, Christopher Yost, and Clayton Crain. *X-Force.* New York: Marvel, 2008. Print.

Kyle, Craig, Christopher Yost, and Clayton Crain. *X-Force.* New York: Marvel, 2009. Print.

Minority Report. Dir. Steven Spielberg. By Philip K. Dick, Scott Frank, and Jon Cohen. Perf. Tom Cruise. Twentieth Century Fox Film Corporation, 2002. Film.

Monsters, Inc. By Peter Docter and David Silverman. Perf. John Goodman, Billy Crystal. Pixar Animation Studios, 2001. DVD.

Morrison, Grant, Leinil Francis. Yu, Igor Kordey, Mark Morales, Prentis Rollins, Dan Green, Gerry Alanguilan, Danny Miki, Rich Perotta, Scott Hanna, Sandu Florea, Brian Haberlin, Sciver Ethan. Van, Frank Quitely, Tony Harris, and T. Saida. *New X-Men.* New York: Marvel, 2008. Print.

Pak, Greg, Giandomenico Carmine. Di, Matt Hollingsworth, Dave Lanphear, and Natalie Lanphear. *X-Men.* New York: Marvel, 2009. Print.

Peter Pan. Prod. Walt Disney. Perf. Bobby Driscoll. Walt Disney Productions, 1953. DVD.

Star Wars: A New Hope. Dir. George Lucas. By George Lucas, Gilbert Taylor, John Williams, Richard Chew, Paul Hirsch, and Marcia Lucas. Prod. Gary Kurtz and John Barry. Perf. Mark Hamill, Harrison Ford, Carrie Fisher, Peter Cushing, Alec Guinness, and Anthony Daniels. Twentieth Century-Fox Film Corporation, 1977. DVD.

Star Wars: Return of the Jedi. Dir. Richard Marquand. By Lawrence Kasdan and George Lucas. Perf. Mark Hamill, Harrison Ford, Carrie Fisher, and Billy Dee Williams. Twentieth Century-Fox Film Corp., 1983. Film.

Star Wars: The Empire Strikes Back. Dir. Irvin Kershner. By Leigh Brackett and Lawrence Kasdan. Perf. Mark Hamill, Harrison Ford, Carrie Fisher, and Billy Dee Williams. Twentieth Century-Fox Film Corporation, 1980. Film.

Toy Story. By John Lasseter. Perf. Tom Hanks, Tim Allen. Pixar Animation Studios, 1995. DVD.

The Transformers: The Movie. Dir. Nelson Shin. By Ron Friedman. Perf. Leonard Nimoy, Judd Nelson, Eric Idle, Robert Stack. Sunbow Productions, 1986. Film.

Watterson, Bill. "Calvin & Hobbes." Comic strip. Print.

World Wrestling Entertainment. "RAW." *RAW*. Television.

World Wrestling Entertainment. "Smackdown." *Smackdown*. Television.

Yost, Christopher, Trevor Hairsine, Kris Justice, Sean McKeever, Mike Mayhew, Mike Carey, J. K. Woodward, Kieron Gillen, Dan Panosian, Mark Texeira, David Yardin, and Ibraim Roberson. *X-Men*. New York: Marvel, 2009. Print.